T0381139

MY ANSWERS TO QUESTIONS

BILL AUBUCHON

© Copyright 2024 *Bill Aubuchon*.

All rights reserved. No part of this publication may be reproduced, stored in a retrieval system, or transmitted, in any form or by any means, electronic, mechanical, photocopying, recording, or otherwise, without the written prior permission of the author.

Order this book online at www.trafford.com
or email orders@trafford.com

Most Trafford titles are also available at major online book retailers.

 www.trafford.com

North America & international
toll-free: 844 688 6899 (USA & Canada)
fax: 812 355 4082

Our mission is to efficiently provide the world's finest, most comprehensive book publishing service, enabling every author to experience success. To find out how to publish your book, your way, and have it available worldwide, visit us online at www.trafford.com

Because of the dynamic nature of the Internet, any web addresses or links contained in this book may have changed since publication and may no longer be valid. The views expressed in this work are solely those of the author and do not necessarily reflect the views of the publisher, and the publisher hereby disclaims any responsibility for them.

Any people depicted in stock imagery provided by Getty Images are models, and such images are being used for illustrative purposes only.
Certain stock imagery © Getty Images.

ISBN: 978-1-6987-1727-2 (sc)
ISBN: 978-1-6987-1729-6 (hc)
ISBN: 978-1-6987-1728-9 (e)

Library of Congress Control Number: 2024914499

Print information available on the last page.

Trafford rev. 10/11/2024

Contents

Have you ever won anything?

Yes … I've "won" through others.

I first "won" on my wedding day marrying Karson Young on July 9, 1972 in Ross, California … now over 50 years ago!

I also "won" on the birthdays of our two incredible children … Marin and Will!

I "won" again when the two children married two fabulous spouses … Jim and Gretchen!

And, I "won" a final time with five awesome grandchildren … THE FAB FIVE … Charlotte and Tyler (twins), Liam, Burke and Lucy!

What qualities do you most value in your friends?

I value most that they are first my friends … that they put up with me … and that they're always there when I need them to listen. Quality-wise I value, in no particular order:

- – Integrity
- – Courage
- – Kindness
- – a Sense of Humor
- – Humility

At what times in your life were you the happiest, and why?

––––•┉╫┉•––––

Nothing makes me more grateful as when I'm "In the Moment" with my family … that they're all happy and that I'm hopefully contributing to a better life in general for them … just allowing them to see the best of themselves!

What also gives me satisfaction is when I'm in the flow of trying to get something done in an analog kind of way because I don't have a lot of technical ability … taking a walk … reading a newspaper … handwriting a thank you note or sympathy card … harvesting grapes in September … networking with young business people … co-authoring a business math book with my cousin (years ago) …

Have you pulled any great pranks?

I'm not really a prankster but I've been involved in playing a couple of practical jokes.

One was a little mischievous and required a community effort in that it took everyone on a college dorm floor to "brick-up" a proctor's door at night while he was sleeping … BIG SURPRISE in the morning when he opened his door!

One was more of a teasing hoax when I was young during the holidays … putting a Wal-Mart sweater in a Lord & Taylor box to get back at a then annoying "fashionista" sister.

One was a bit of a literal "put-on" … wearing a magnetic fake diamond stud earring and walking into a room of pretty conservative family members. I had a good time observing reactions for about a half-hour until I just reached-up and pulled off the earring … good laughs all around.

What is one of your fondest childhood memories?

That's easy.

My #1 favorite memory as a kid was Summer days at "CAMP".

The Aubuchon Family Camp on Wyman's Pond in Westminster was purchased in 1930 by my Grandfather and his brother John. It was a great Summer escape place for my Dad, his siblings and cousins when they were young and for us when we were young.

Swimming … water-skiing … playing volleyball and horseshoes … cookouts … eating watermelon and roasting marshmallows … (maybe even getting to sleep over and eating Mémère's famous crepes in the morning).

Just being together with all our cousins … growing up together with family traditions and values … it was "THE BEST OF TIMES" … full of bright promise!

What is one of your favorite trips that you've taken? What made it great?

My favorite trip is always the trip HOME(S) … Rockport, MA … Nokomis, FL … Comptche, CA

Why? Being with and always grateful for family and friends … and making great memories!

(Of course, after waking up in the morning and getting to the kitchen to make a pot of coffee is a pretty good trip too).

What is one of the bravest things you've ever done, and what was the outcome?

We usually think of brave people as those who respond instantly and courageously in moments of fear and uncertainty … soldiers … police/fire … health care workers … educators. I'm NOT one of these fantastic folks.

I think people can also be brave by just "Showing Up" (80% of life according to Woody Allen) … "Being Present" … being who they are and doing something where there are no guarantees except maybe the likelihood of failure.

For me it was leaving the security of a good job to risk an entrepreneurial adventure.

The outcome? Gaining 2 aspirational qualities: being real and being vulnerable.

What is your idea of perfect happiness?

—•◀|||▶•—

As I answered on page 4 … to be "In the Moment" … being mindful … being intentional … being responsible … hanging out with family … listening to them … focusing … knowing they're happy, healthy, feeling safe and having fun.

I'm also happy and grateful when I think I've made good choices … when I've been given the opportunity to contribute … and when I've cared well for those I love.

That's truly THE BEST that life can offer!

Are you more like your father or your mother? In what ways?

I think I'm a bit of a hybrid when it comes to the values both my parents instilled in me and for how those values have influenced how I've tried to conduct my life. (In no particular order):

From Mom:

- Honesty and telling the truth
- Appreciation and gratitude for my blessings
- Humble accomplishment ... never stop learning

From Dad:

- Leadership and teamwork
  ("The collective intelligence of us all!")
- Stewardship and supporting the community at large
- Respect and honor the family heritage

What are your favorite possessions? Why?

Family memories … ALL OF THEM!

Why? That should be pretty obvious.

What do you consider one of your greatest achievements in life?

Other than marrying Karson Young … making the positive choices I made … choices that helped shape me into who I am:

- Being open-minded and balanced
- Being generous with time and talent
- Being decent … honest … kind
- "Showing Up" to life's events
- Having the right values and trying hard to live by them

Tell me about one of the best days you can remember.

Buying my first car … a pre-owned, 1966, short-throw shifter, yellow, MGB convertible.

Top down … music cranking!

It pointed to a specific time in life and a feeling of freedom … downright exhilarating!

Have you ever given or been the recipient of a random act of kindness?

ON THE RECEIVING END: In the long-ago days when cash was predominant and where I didn't check my wallet before leaving for the grocery store did I find myself "short" when someone in back of me in the check-out line "covered" me with a $5 bill.

That gesture was more kind and generous than I had any right to expect.

ON THE GIVING END: I enjoy showing up to events and, without obligation, give out bottles of Docker Hill Pinot Noir.

It's pretty well received.

What is one of the strangest things that has ever happened to you?

Well … nothing like being "beamed-up" into an alien spacecraft or seeing the ghost of a past relative but … it was like looking into the mirror … a "doppelganger" …

When I was younger and walking on a sidewalk in Boston I passed my "double". He was even dressed like me.

Even though we noticed each other in utter amazement, we didn't stop to chat or simply be amused by this incredible coincidence … we simply went our separate ways.

Still … pretty surreal.

(I sometimes wonder where he is today).

How did you feel when your first child was born?

Watching your children (1st or 2nd) being born in the hospital … it's such an honor … PURE BLISS!

(I even got to like changing a filled, piping-hot diaper).

I'm so proud of both our children … they're JUST WONDERS!

The one thing I'd like most to be remembered for is being a great Dad.

What would you consider
your motto?

I'm not big on mottoes but if I had one it might look like this … life is determined by the CHOICES you make (in no particular order):

- "Showing Up"
- Being purposeful
- Making an effort
- Being respectful of others
- "Being yourself … everyone else is already taken" (THANKS Oscar Wilde)
- Allowing people to see the best of themselves
- Not trading on what you know personally about anyone
- Taking a stand for what's right
- Having the right values (and trying hard to live by them … not easy)

(Of course, the NFL Patriots draft-picking #199 in 2000 proved to be a good choice too).

Which fads did you embrace while growing up?

Growing up was a special time!

When I could make them I was all over the Saturday night, high school "Sock Hops" and early rock 'n' roll.

I loved my Madras button-down, short-sleeve shirts. (I still do!)

I had an 8-track in the car.

I brought a bean-bag chair for the college dorm room.

I did some college "streaking" in the secret "Nude Olympics".

In general it was about the music … (on vinyl of course … 45's and 78's).

What is one of the most selfless things you have done in life?

Answering a previous question on page 19 about being on the receiving end of a random act of kindness, I've passed on that kindness (paying the "short" for someone ahead of me in line at the grocery store).

I'm up to 2 "short-covers" and counting.

Do something for someone who couldn't possibly repay you.

When I was working and visiting stores I would bring a bag of donuts and a "Box of Joe" for the early morning store crew.

There's a lot of stress today. If you can bring a little laughter to share with others it goes a long way to creating a positive setting.

Selflessness … yes, it surprises and makes other people happy … it makes me happy too!

What are some of your special talents?

I wouldn't call it a "special talent" but, I believe I have an understanding of how important it is to get along with people.

EVERYONE has to be respected, understood, appreciated and accepted …

> For who they are … their diversity …

> For what they stand for and believe in …

> For how they came to believe what they do …

> For where they come from …

> For what they hope for!

Did you consider any other careers? How did you choose?

I started my work career as an Instructor of Marketing at Quinnipiac College (now University) in Hamden, CT from 1968-1971.

I interrupted my long-term work career with Aubuchon Hardware when I started a mail-order company (The Princeton Company) from 1975-1981.

It wasn't successful but it was very instructive and humbling.

My true second act came in 2008 when I really took "the road less traveled" (THANKS Robert Frost) and started Docker Hill Vineyard in Comptche, CA.

While there was a little second-guessing at first about making this choice, it's turning out to be a very important part of my life, and like I said before on page 23 … life is about the CHOICES we make and the character narratives we craft with those choices.

You have to embrace growing wine grapes as being high on joy and passion and low on profitability.

What advice do you wish you had taken from your parents?

I had taken most of the advice my parents had given me. It was good advice and I never regretted getting any of it.

However, I never thought that if I didn't take their advice that I'd somehow be doomed to a life of drug dependency and crime.

Because of them I've learned to be happy vs. unhappy … to be optimistic vs. cynical … to find reasons to laugh more … to enjoy life vs. finding reasons not to.

What have been some of your life's greatest surprises?

Some of the best surprises I've had have come from unexpected phone calls or visits from friends … old and new.

But … the #1 surprise (NO CONTEST) in my life was when we, as a family, were vacationing in Puerto Rico celebrating my 60th birthday … well, that's what I thought.

At breakfast the next morning my daughter Marin distributes envelopes inviting all of us her wedding THAT AFTERNOON ON THE BEACH!

I was absolutely frozen in my seat … speechless, for what some say, was an hour.

We knew Jim for some time and were absolutely thrilled for the both of them.

SURPRISED? Yes … Dad was REALLY SURPRISED!

What is one of your favorite children's stories?

I can't say there was just "one".

From early childhood I remember *The Little Engine That Could, The Giving Tree* and *The Little Prince*.

Later on, it was the Mark Twain and Robert Louis Stevenson books.

And, in adolescence, it was *The Diary of Anne Frank, To Kill a Mockingbird* and *The Catcher in the Rye*.

Children's books speak to being courageous … to being funny … to being empathetic … to being hopeful.

What advice would you give your great grandchildren?

Adopt an "Attitude of Gratitude".

Fully appreciate not only the blessings and privileges you have but, more importantly, those family members who preceded you. They sacrificed a lot to give you those advantages.

In return, practice small, and sometimes random, acts of kindness to those you know and to complete strangers.

Being appreciative and grateful will make you happy and give you positive well-being.

What inventions have had the biggest impact on your day-to-day life?

At my Bachelor Party in 1972 the guys chipped–in and bought me a Commodore "Pocket" Calculator.

You had to have had a BIG pocket to put that Calculator into. Price: $250!

In the early 80's, I got a Motorola Mobile Phone. Weight: about 2 lbs.!

Today, I don't know where I'd be without my iPhone and chromebook.

What are some of the choices you made in raising your children?

To impress upon them:

1. That they owed us nothing. It was our choice to bring them into the world. It was therefore our obligation to love them and provide for them … that THEIR needs and aspirations were the most important.

2. That life is indeed about choices and that they're responsible for making those choices and the consequences that come with those choices.

3. That they couldn't be happy 100% of the time … that things happen not how we wish or hope they would be. No life is free of twists and turns and challenges.

   That said, they can choose to be happy in an imperfect world.

4. That their lives should be lived without an entitled attitude but rather with commitment, determination, grit and fortitude.

THEY'VE BOTH MADE US VERY PROUD!

Who is the wisest person you've known? What have you learned from them?

I've known many wise people from whom I've learned much.

If I had to choose one, I would choose a high school English teacher … Edward Powers.

The lesson from Mr. Powers was MUTUAL RESPECT.

It starts with actively listening to understand … being curious and showing a genuine interest in what people think … appreciating where their opinions come from and why those opinions matter to them.

When relationships are challenged and perspectives contested by different points of view, can we focus on what might bring us together? … can we find some "common ground"?

Finding that "common ground" (what unites us more than divides us) at least gives us a chance to then bring people together to discuss the flashpoints that drive us apart.

THANK YOU, Mr. Powers.

Who inspires you?

There are many people who are inspiring. But, for me, it's my children and grandchildren.

Listening to them … laughing and sharing … being patient with each other … being kind with one another … enjoying each other in a loving spirit.

It's like watching a garden bloom!

What is your view of success?

Success is a TODAY, live-in-the-moment mindset.

Success is always available and not some vision of a destination.

Frame success in the NOW, not the next.

It doesn't make sense to rob ourselves of the enjoyment of TODAY for a tomorrow we don't know yet.

So … set yourself up to "Be Present" … to "Show Up" … to "Be Positive" … to "Be Curious"… to "Be Joyous" … to "Be True To Yourself" … you're much more than what you can't do or don't have.

Connect with people TODAY that give you peace, joy, love and an inspired attitude.

That's SUCCESS … a sense of purpose … a state of being … a way of living … TODAY!

What is your favorite joke?

It's more of a quote than a joke.

It's one I've used often but it was particularly appropriate for my cousin's eulogy.

It's attributed to the late Groucho Marx:

A GOOD friend would bail you out of jail … but your BEST friend would be the one sitting next to you in the cell saying … "Damn … that was AWESOME!"

If you could choose any talents to have, what would they be?

I suspect that most people answering this question would say something like … an ability to:

-   Play a musical instrument, or
-   Be fluent in a certain language, or
-   Score your age in a round of golf

I want to develop the ability to display calm and adaptability "In the Moment" when it's both important and difficult …

"In the Moment" of challenge or opportunity … discovering how to change when change is hardest.

Like those other aspirational talents, this can be learned.

All it takes is practice.

What are your favorite memories of each of your children growing up?

Our children gave us great joy and pride every day when they were growing up. We love them both very much.

So … there are many, many wonderful memories. Favorites? Here are some (but certainly not all):

MARIN:

- Class President in all of her primary school grades
- Captain of her Field Hockey and Lacrosse teams
- A college extracurricular activity that landed her first, and only, job … the day after graduation
- That job led to her owning today her own live music booking and marketing company

WILL:

- Making a wooden airplane in the garage at age 3 (it was going to fly)
- Overcoming a speech impediment by age 8

- Qualifying for the Junior Olympics as a member of the Mt. Wachusett Ski Team
- Today, he is the 4th generation CEO of the family consumer hardware business

What do you think is the meaning of life?

Well, that's something people have answered on multiple levels … philosophically, theologically, existentially, etc.

To me what matters most in life is to be RESILIENT and to be ALWAYS LEARNING.

When I think of resiliency, I think about a Christmas toy I received when I was young … a Popeye Inflatable Punching Bag. You'd knock Popeye down, but he'd always bounce back up from the floor.

Life will throw us uncertain, challenging situations … even unsuccessful outcomes.

Being resilient (i.e., knowing your purpose … your "why", staying optimistic, being adaptable … navigating the challenges, etc.) allows you to adjust your response, "bounce back" better and fortifies your character.

Cue Friedrich Nietzsche … "What doesn't kill you makes you stronger".

There's nothing sweeter than achieving something important, or overcoming some adversity, when you've really, really paid the price.

And … I want to be in contact with people and contexts that lift me up and make me feel terrific about life's possibilities … as I would wish for them.

I want to feel that I'm staying curious … eager to keep learning … evolving.

Today is not the same as yesterday … I'll be different in the future.

I want to find out what that change is going to be.

Do you have a favorite poem? What is it?

I'm not sure they would qualify as acknowledged poems by experts but one is from part of a public address that President Theodore Roosevelt delivered in Paris on April 23, 1910 called *The Man in the Arena*.

It's about life being neither a success nor a failure. It's about getting up with grit ... being weathered by hard work and valiant effort ... "Showing Up" and "Being Present" ... being ALL IN!

The other is a quote from Scottish author Robert Louis Stevenson about again the meaning of success in life ... *That Man is a Success* ... "Who looked for the best in others and gave the best he had".

It's not related to monetary wealth but for appreciation and gratitude in life!

What do you most dislike?

I dislike the dogmatic imposition of moral certitude and hypocritical righteous rhetoric by ideologues of all stripes … conservative nationalists or liberal secularists … an absolute intolerance for another perspective.

Put another way, I dislike it when we can't see around our differences and, as a consequence, legitimate, good–faith conversation doesn't make space for contrary viewpoints and ends up, potentially, poisoning relationships.

I dislike it when liars and bullies suffer no consequences.

I dislike it when arrogance and egotism, in whatever guise they wear, go unchecked.

What do you do for fun?

Well … it can be many things depending on your age.

When I was young it was bicycling to Goodrich Park to play stickball with friends.

Later, it was basketball … in high school and college.

Today, it's getting together with old and new friends in ROMEO (Retired Old Men Eating Out) groups, sharing life stories and discussing things folks want to talk about.

We "Show Up" for one another and enjoy each other's company.

Like those early stickball days, it's an obligation I have with others.

You have to make room for fun … it's got to be intentional … on the calendar in pen (not pencil)!

How should you handle
getting older?

I've learned to appreciate the person I've become ... weathered yes, but the source of my present well-being and happiness.

Our bodies aren't built to last forever ... it's a privilege to grow old.

Are you happy with the life you've lived? ... staying resilient and relevant? ... seizing the opportunity(s) to learn and still be more? ... building a supportive community?

You don't think you're getting older if you explore what else you can be. Have purpose ... where do you find meaning?

Reverse the thinking that says there's more behind you than in front of you ... pursue the "now".

Establish positive attitudes and habits and stay true to who you are ... value your worth.

And then, there's THE FAB FIVE (our grandchildren) ... they lighten my step, warm my heart and enrich my soul!

And please … don't make your age someone else's problem … recognize the things you really can't change by accepting help with grace, humility and gratitude.

Let go of the chagrin.

It's about letting those who care about us know not only who we were but, as important, who we still are.

(Oh#1 … a strong sense of humor and not taking ourselves at all seriously are definitely big pluses!).

(Oh#2 … if you get a chance … buy a Porsche … this one is timelessly analog with a 6-speed manual gearbox!).

What simple pleasures of life do you truly enjoy?

Feeling good after a morning walk. Yes … it's got body benefits but for me it's also an opportunity to be "mindful" and to stimulate ideas.

Drinking a glass (or 2) of good Docker Hill Pinot Noir.

Making people laugh.

Watching the sunset and stars come out on the decks in Rockport and Docker Hill.

Best of all … great, satisfying relationships with family and friends … because everyone is dependent on the support of others.

Social connections matter!

How is life different today compared to when you were a child?

Well … I'm not sure the TV days of "Ozzie and Harriet" (my early years) ever reflected the reality of the late 1950's, but the post-W.W. II values espoused in the show grounded many people at that time.

Maybe I'm wrong but it made for a seemingly simpler time … a time of stability and security … we felt grounded.

Today … it's the challenge of technology and the digitization of nearly everything. It has the power to change things completely … and quickly.

Today … it's the speed and influence of social media … mostly positive but also, in my view, negative (i.e., limiting person-to-person interaction that teaches people how to be socially and culturally connected, to become good citizens and be civically engaged).

Today … it's the proliferation of curated news and information through cable channels, streaming services and the Internet as compared to the 3 national, black-and-white TV networks in the 1950's and 1960's.

Today … it's, sadly, a loss of civility and mutual respect in the public square with regards things political, cultural, religious, racial and more. Something's been lost in the ways in which we relate with each other when emotions run high.

Do you have any particularly vivid memories of your grandparents?

There are many wonderful memories of my 4 Grandparents.

Two are noteworthy of my Grandfathers.

My Pépère Corriveau was a proud French-Canadian immigrant. He founded The Corriveau Insurance Company in Nashua, NH in 1912. It's still operating today. He was also elected the Registrar of Deeds for Hillsborough County for 30+ years.

After Thanksgiving dinner each year, I remember him walking to the dining room cupboard and taking out a bottle of Seagram's Crown Royal in the purple bag. He would ceremoniously pull apart the tasseled drawstring, pull out the bottle and pour each adult a shot glass of Crown Royal. (I got the purple bag to put my marbles in).

I believe it symbolized his rightfully-earned sense of achievement as an immigrant American.

My Pépère Aubuchon, also a proud French-Canadian immigrant, was the ultimate serial entrepreneur. After founding The Aubuchon Hardware Company in Fitchburg, MA in 1908, he went on to start

The Aubuchon Funeral Home, with his brother John (1914), The Aubuchon Realty Co., Inc. (1932), The Westminster Silver Fox Farm (1940), Standard Sash & Door Co., Inc. (1941), Beaver Investment Company (1960) and Snowflake Wash & Dry, Inc. (1961).

All this from someone with only a 5th grade education!

The Hardware and Realty Companies are very successfully operating today under 4th generation family management and ownership.

He'd be so proud!

What have you changed your mind about over the years?

⫘⫘

Realizing that the more you think you know … the more you know that you know very little.

Realizing that life is more than just circumstance or luck (though a little luck is appreciated). Life is about push and pull, hard work, making room for mistakes and learning from them and above all … being in touch with what makes me "tick" and, most importantly, its effect on others … being self-aware.

Realizing that getting older doesn't have to be feared or dreaded as long as you have positivity about ageism … avoid negative mental and physical messages … build existing relationships … forge new friendships.

AMBITION … at first it was all about getting to a specific place(s). Now, it's much broader as in how I want to live, work and connect with people. (And "staying salty").

GRATITUDE … commemorating what earlier family generations sacrificed to make my life, and the life of my family, easier.

Which word(s) or phrase(s) do you most overuse?

THANK YOU! … (a SINCERE Thank You!)

I appreciate EVERYONE who deserves our gratitude.

Especially so are those who made and make a difference in our life … those who mattered … those who helped us take the next step.

If genuine, and meant to make someone feel recognized and valued, THANK YOU has the power of positivity.

Thank You!

Has anyone ever rescued you, figuratively or literally?

YES … I was literally rescued from falling backwards off a cliff in 2001 in Vail, CO by my good friend Wells Dow.

We were out to attend Wells' daughter Alicia's wedding and the day before we rented bicycles to take a run through Glenwood Canyon on the way to a picnic.

I somehow managed to slide off the bike path and went head-over-heals.

I got up pretty dazed and was heading backwards towards the edge of the cliff when Wells grabbed my T-shirt collar and pulled me back from sure disaster.

The local hospital ER staff got me patched up.

Today, scars are a permanent "tattoo reminder" of that eventful day … they remind me to respect the moment-to-moment experiences life can serve up … both positive and negative.

(The rental bike was "totaled". I paid for its replacement).

THANK YOU Wells.

How should someone handle regret?

There's really nothing you can do about what you've already done or the list of self-limiting "could-a-beens"/"should-a-beens".

All we can do is learn, make better choices and give ourselves a chance for better outcomes.

Meanwhile … be good to yourself and maintain a sense of humor and humility.

I'm not interested in some nostalgic version of who I once was. I'm more interested in who I've become, where I am now and where I'm going … no "Glory Days" storytelling. (THANKS Bruce Springsteen).

Let's not torture ourselves with things we might have said or didn't do or allow the past to get in the way of a positive future … aka the rest of our lives!

Who have been your closest friends throughout the years?

Aside from my immediate family and my cousin Marcus, who I considered another brother for 70+ years, my closest friends have been my high school classmates … for all of 60+ years. We have mutual goodwill toward each other.

We trust and respect each other's beliefs and values … we're concerned for each other's well–being.

We appreciate and feel comfortable going with our natural inclinations … good and bad.

We reunion twice a year … once in Massachusetts and once in Florida.

When together, we're engaged and truly enjoy each other's company.

The best friendships are ends in themselves.

What would you consider the most overrated virtue(s)?

Virtue (i.e., being kind, being generous, being honest) itself is not overrated. What we mistake for virtue is:

- The notion of perfection. It gets in the way of "the possible". Accept the ambiguity life will throw you. Then favor timely action and reevaluate based on results. Perfectionistic attitudes also have the ability to alienate everyone who are not so inclined.
- The notion of honor … especially when it's weaponized to hurt, or worse, someone.
- The notion of entitlement when what's needed is a sense of purpose … what we do for others … helping people walk through life … servanthood.
- The notion of moderation … especially when it comes to Scotch.

What things do you think you cannot live without?

Having purpose (a "why") and a positive attitude.

Connective relationships of all types … spouse, children, son-in law, daughter-in-law, grandchildren, friends, neighbors, parents, grandparents, extended family, work associates.

They're the foundation of happiness.

If other things are meant to come my way, they will … what's not, won't … and it won't matter.

(Of course, a good cup of morning coffee would be hard to live without too).

How would you like to
be remembered?

I don't think about whether people will remember me or not because sooner or later I'll be forgotten for what I might have said or did … and that's fine.

It was my decision to put in the years of effort, the travel, the time away from the family. A cost had to be exacted and I was willing to exact it … no one wants to be remembered for that.

What ultimately matters is that they feel I was a good steward of what was entrusted to me … a family, a business, a piece of land. (THANKS Maya Angelou).

It was a privilege … the most divine thing I can think of.

On what occasion would you lie?

OK … for me outright and intentional lying is not the same as being "less-than-candid".

So, I would be "less-than-candid" when, being totally candid, could be hurtful to anyone I love and care about.

Cue Billy Crystal … "YOU LOOK MARVELOUS!"

What gets you out of bed in the morning?

You mean something other than my OAB (Overactive Bladder) at age 80?

Something perhaps along the lines of passion, purpose, focus, intention, intrinsic motivation or meaning?

Something that brings me satisfaction? Carpe Diem … "Own the Day"?

Well, truthfully, ALL the above with regards family … friends … professional obligations.

I've got a pretty positive attitude … I anticipate positive, quality things happening daily!

What is your favorite trait/ characteristic of each of your 5 grandchildren?

THE FAB FIVE … they're just WONDERFUL!

Many share the same great traits but here I go, cautiously, with what I see today as unique to each:

Charlotte: Accepting … Kindness … Supportive

Tyler: Accomplishing … Self-Confident … Encouraging

Liam: Responsible … Dependable … Cautious

Burke: Self-Disciplined … Diligent … Focused

Lucy: Determined … Fearless … Social

Koko and Aubie are not here to give any of our grandchildren advice or to correct them. That's for their parents.

We're here to love them beyond question, celebrate them and cheer them on to be the happy and successful people they will become.

Any favorite social media platforms ... websites, podcasts, apps?

NONE.

I have to admit that I'm a bit tactile about many things:

- Printed, paper newspapers (*The New York Times, The Wall Street Journal.,* and the local daily) keep me updated and balanced wherever I find myself
- Reading hand-held, hard-cover books that get my red-pen underlines, yellow-highlights and dog-eared pages
- Handwriting and mailing THANK YOU notes and sympathy cards
- Reading paper maps
- Handwriting and mailing checks to make payments
- Going to the bank in person. Lisa is very personable and answers my questions face-to-face
- Searching through a printed Dictionary or Thesaurus
- Writing appointments/commitments on a paper calendar
- Hand-winding my square-faced, 1973 Girard-Perregaux watch

- Having my grandchildren dial-up a classic, wall-mounted, landline rotary phone at Docker Hill
- Driving my 2000, stick-shift, VW Cabrio convertible

Living to scroll through apps and watch YouTube videos helps to contribute to life's problems …

(OK … definitely an exaggeration … but you get my point).

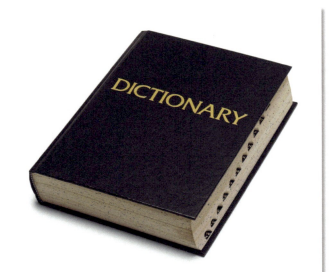

You're organizing a restaurant dinner party. If you could, which people, alive or dead, do you invite?

It depends …

on where we're eating …

and who's picking up the check.

What's on your nightstand?

Some people might want to impress you by listing a stack of book titles authored by people you've never heard of.

For me … it's a lighted analog alarm clock and the control for my electric blanket.

I'd fall asleep reading the back of a cereal box.

Finally ... any hard-life lessons to pass on?

–•◀|||▶•–

YES ... in no particular order:

1. As tempting as it might be, you can't fix other peoples' problems ... no matter how sincere your intentions ... it's not your job to try and make other people happy.

2. Don't portray yourself as a victim (i.e., self-pity) ... take ownership of your situation ... only you can do this ... (and it's on YOU).

3. The "80–20 Rule" (i.e., that roughly 80% of effects/outcomes come from 20% of causes/sources) applies to nearly everything in life.

4. Failing ≠ Failure. Don't be so afraid of failing that you fail to try ... you can't be a champ without the chance of being a chump ... take a shot and ride out the consequences (and keep learning).

5. Always deliver on the promises you make ... be congruent ... that is your say/do ratio is 1-to-1.

6. Play the long game ... trade short-term expedient gains for long-term value benefits ... success is a lifelong journey.

7. Understand that you can do all the right things and still not get what you're looking for (ex., you don't get the job you thought you just "bagged") … it could be timing, luck, personal chemistry … let it go … it's life … it's temporary … move on.

8. People don't notice you as much as you think (they're more interested in their favorite subject: themselves) so … put ego in its place … humility (a quiet, underrated strength) doesn't mean thinking less of yourself … it means thinking of yourself less … character matters!

9. Learn the dignity of work no matter how routine, mundane or tedious … it's an education no money can buy and no school can teach.

10. Don't disrespect people you don't understand … listen to learn without judgement … give people the gift of your attention to connect … it might be they know something you don't.

11. What you decide NOT to do or say matters as much as what you decide to do or say.

Printed in the United States
by Baker & Taylor Publisher Services